MW01489929

Rooted In Christ:

A Journey of Faith, Growth, & Purpose

Sharon G. Carineau

This book or parts thereof may not be reproduced in any form, stored in a retrieval system, or transmitted in any form by any means—electronic, mechanical, photocopying, recording, or otherwise—without prior written permission of the publisher. For permission requests, please email the published at carineausharon@gmail.com

Acknowledgments

I express my deepest gratitude to the Almighty God, the source of all wisdom and inspiration, for guiding me through the creation of this work. Your divine presence has been my constant source of strength and inspiration, shaping every word and thought.

I extend heartfelt thanks to my friends and family for their support and understanding while writing this book. I am profoundly grateful for your encouragement and love.

Finally, to the readers who embark on this journey, may these words be a source of inspiration and encouragement. Your openness to explore the depths of faith is a testament to the enduring power of the Christian journey. May this work serve as a blessing and inspiration to all who engage with its pages. To God be the glory, both now and forevermore. Amen

Contents

Introduction

Welcome to "Rooted in Christ: A Journey of Faith, Growth, and Purpose." In the following pages, we embark on a life-changing exploration of what it truly means to be deeply rooted in Jesus Christ.

Purpose of the Book

The purpose of this book is to guide you on a journey of faith, growth, and purpose rooted in the teachings of Jesus Christ. We will explore the fundamental principles of cultivating a strong spiritual foundation, nurturing a profound relationship with Christ, and allowing the power of grace to shape our character. As we navigate the chapters, we will delve into the spiritual fruits that emerge from a life grounded in Christ, face trials with resilience and trust, and discover the joy of embracing our uniquely tailored purpose. This journey is not just about personal transformation; it extends to our broader purpose in God's grand design. We will explore how a life rooted in Christ equips us to live purposefully, utilizing our unique gifts and talents for the greater good. Along the way, we'll encounter practices that foster spiritual growth, address doubts that may arise, and offer a vision for sustaining a lifelong relationship with Christ. As you embark on this expedition through the pages of "Rooted in Christ," my hope is that you will find inspiration, guidance, and encouragement to deepen your connection with Christ. May this exploration lead you to a more profound understanding of your purpose, a strengthened faith in the face of adversity, and a life that bears the fruits of love, joy, and peace. The journey begins here as we delve into the importance of being rooted in Christ.

The Importance of Being Rooted

Life is filled with storms, uncertainties, and challenges that threaten to uproot us. In the face of these trials, our foundation sustains us, providing strength, resilience, and unwavering hope. This foundation is none other than Christ himself, the cornerstone upon which our faith stands firm. As we delve into the essence of being rooted in Christ, we will uncover the profound impact this connection can have on every aspect of our lives.

Chapter One

Call to the Roots

Establishing The Foundation

Roots emerge as a powerful metaphor, symbolizing the unseen yet foundational aspects of our spiritual journey. This chapter marks the beginning of our exploration into being rooted in Christ, a journey that beckons us to establish a firm foundation in the rich soil of Christ's teachings, love, and power.

The Metaphor of Roots

"So that Christ may dwell in your hearts through faith. And I pray that you, being rooted and established in love." Ephesians 3:17 (NIV)

The metaphor of roots, as expressed in *Ephesians 3:17*, unveils a profound understanding of the relationship between our faith and the indwelling presence of Christ in our hearts. The imagery of roots is a poetic representation, capturing the essence of the depth, stability, and permanence of our connection with Him. In the natural world, roots are the unseen anchors that provide stability and nourishment to a plant. Similarly, in the spiritual realm, our faith is the unseen but vital connection that attaches us to the source of life—Christ Himself. The metaphor of roots emphasizes not just a fleeting connection or a surface-level belief but a deep, embedded, and foundational relationship with Jesus Christ. When Paul prays for the Ephesian believers to be "rooted and established in love," he invokes an image of spiritual grounding. Just as roots firmly anchor a plant in the soil, our faith, rooted in love, anchors us in Christ. This grounding is not temporary or subject to life's shifting circumstances; instead, it reflects a firm and unshakable foundation built on the enduring love of God. Being rooted in Christ provides endless nourishment. Just as roots draw sustenance from the soil, our faith draws strength and vitality from the love of Christ. The deeper our roots go into the soil of His love, the more nourished and resilient our faith becomes, enabling us to withstand the storms of life.

Furthermore, the image of being "rooted and established in love" suggests growth and maturity. A well-rooted plant survives and thrives, producing fruit and blossoming in its season. A faith fastened in the love of Christ has the potential to grow, mature, and bear the fruits of the Spirit—love, joy, peace, patience, kindness, goodness, faithfulness, gentleness, and self-control *(Galatians 5:22-23)*. The metaphor of roots in *Ephesians 3:17* invites us to contemplate the depth of our connection with Christ. It challenges us to examine the strength of our faith, urging us to ensure that our roots are not shallow or easily uprooted but deeply embedded in the rich soil of His enduring and unwavering love. Being rooted in Christ is not a passive state but an active and ongoing journey of deepening our faith and intimacy with the One who is the true source of life and love.

The Importance of Spiritual Foundations

"Therefore, everyone who hears these words of mine and puts them into practice is like a wise man who built his house on the rock. The rain came down, the streams rose, and the winds blew and beat against that house, yet it did not fall because it had its foundation on the rock."

Matthew 7:24-25 (NIV)

In the timeless parable of the wise builder found in *Matthew 7:24-25*, Jesus masterfully imparts a profound lesson about the indispensable significance of a solid foundation in our spiritual journey. The analogy of building a house upon a rock serves as a powerful metaphor for the spiritual foundations we establish in our lives. Jesus begins by emphasizing the vital action of not just hearing His words but putting them into practice. This combination of hearing and applying signifies an active engagement with the teachings of Christ. It mirrors being rooted in Him, where our faith is not merely theoretical but manifests in our daily actions and choices. The choice of a rock as the foundation is deliberate; rocks are enduring, unyielding, and unwavering against external pressures. By comparing the wise builder to someone who builds on a rock, Jesus emphasizes the need for a foundation that can withstand the storms of life—rain, rising streams, and fierce winds. Life's storms are unavoidable; they come in various forms—troubles, uncertainties, and adversities.

Yet, the key takeaway from this parable is the resilience and steadfastness of the house built on the rock. Despite the external pressures, it remains unshaken and unbroken. The spiritual parallel is evident: Being rooted in Christ is akin to building our spiritual house upon the rock. Christ, the unchanging and solid foundation, provides stability and strength amidst life's tumultuous circumstances. When our faith is anchored in Him, we gain the capacity to weather the storms with courage. The importance of spiritual foundations compels us to reflect on the substance of our faith. Are we building our lives on the unshakable truth of God's Word, or are we constructing our spiritual house on shifting sands? The call to establish our foundation on the rock challenges us to prioritize a deep and authentic relationship with Christ—beyond mere acknowledgment to active obedience and application of His teachings. Ultimately, we all have a call to be wise builders, intentional about our spiritual foundations. By choosing the rock of Christ, we ensure that our faith is resilient and capable of standing firm, unyielding, and unbroken when the storms of life inevitably come our way.

Responding to the Call

"But blessed is the one who trusts in the Lord, whose confidence is in him. They will be like a tree planted by the water that sends out its roots by the stream. It does not fear when heat comes; its leaves are always green. It has no worries in a year of drought and never fails to bear fruit."

Jeremiah 17:7-8 (NIV)

Jeremiah 17:7-8 extends a compelling invitation—to respond to the call of placing our trust in the Lord, securing our confidence in Him. The response to trusting in the Lord is depicted as being like a tree planted by water, carrying many blessings and assurances that resonate through the imagery of a flourishing tree. Trusting in the Lord is not merely an acknowledgment but a profound reliance on His sovereignty and goodness. Answering the call to roots brings blessings and unshakable confidence. Our roots in the Lord grant resilience, perpetual vitality, and the ability to bear fruit even in challenging seasons.

1. Thriving Resilience

The tree planted by the water embodies a resilience that defies external difficulties. Its roots extend deeply, drawing sustenance from the stream. Similarly, when we respond to the call to trust in the Lord, our spiritual roots delve into the fountain of eternal nourishment, granting us the resilience to withstand life's adversities.

2. Perpetual Vitality

Even in the face of heat and drought, the tree's leaves remain green, symbolizing perpetual vitality. Likewise, answering the call to trust in the Lord ensures that our spiritual life is not contingent on external circumstances. Our confidence in Him provides a constant source of strength, vitality, and refreshment.

3. Freedom from Fear

The assurance in the passage declares that the tree "does not fear when heat comes." Responding to the call to trust in the Lord liberates us from fear. The deep-rooted confidence in God's faithfulness dispels anxiety and worry, allowing us to face challenges with steadfast assurance.

4. Uninterrupted Fruitfulness

In a remarkable testament to the resilience of its roots, the tree "never fails to bear fruit." This echoes the promise that a life rooted in trust and confidence in the Lord is marked by uninterrupted fruitfulness. Even in the driest seasons, our lives can bear the fruits of the Spirit, impacting others and glorifying God. Responding to the call to roots is not just a one-time decision but an ongoing posture of trust and confidence in the Lord. The blessings are abundant—a life marked by resilience, perpetual vitality, freedom from fear, and uninterrupted fruitfulness. May you heed the call, responding with faith in the One who plants our roots by the living water.

Chapter Two

Christ The Solid Rock

Christ as the Foundation

"For no one can lay any foundation other than the one already laid, which is Jesus Christ." 1 Corinthians 3:11 (NIV)

The foundation upon which all else stands is none other than Jesus Christ—understanding Christ as the foundation means recognizing Him as the bedrock of our beliefs, the anchor of our souls, and the unchanging origin of our hope. Just as a physical structure relies on a solid foundation to endure the test of time, our spiritual lives find stability and endurance in Jesus Christ. Embracing Christ as the foundation sets the stage for a transformative journey, allowing us to build our lives upon the solid rock that is unshaken by the storms of life.

Building a Strong Spiritual Foundation

As we embrace Christ as our foundation, the natural progression is to build upon this sturdy base. But how do we go about constructing a strong spiritual foundation? This section will provide Biblical insights to fortify your roots in Christ. Foundations are not built in a moment but through intentional, purposeful effort. Cultivating a solid spiritual foundation requires a commitment to the disciplines that strengthen our connection with Christ.

Significance of Prayer

"Do not be anxious about anything, but in every situation, by prayer and petition, with thanksgiving, present your requests to God."

Philippians 4:6 (NIV)

Prayer is the sacred dialogue between the Creator and His creation, expressing our dependence on God. Prayer serves as a direct line of communication with God. Prayer is to your spiritual life what breathing is to your natural life. Prayer moves you from stagnation to speed, delay to destiny, confused to clarity, shallow to deep, and overlooked to overtaking. Through prayer, we communicate our needs and cultivate a personal connection with the One who listens and responds. Prayer is a space where vulnerability meets divine love, and our hearts align with God's will. As we cultivate the habit of prayer, we deepen our connection with Christ, finding solace, guidance, and a sense of intimacy in the presence of our Savior. Prayer is more than a religious ritual; it is a practice that opens the door to intimacy with God. We acknowledge our reliance on His wisdom and provision as we present our concerns and desires before Him. Prayer creates a space for communion, allowing us to experience the peace that surpasses understanding. In the quiet moments of communion with God, we increase our knowledge of Christ and strengthen our relationship with Him.

Significance of Scripture

"Your word is a lamp for my feet, a light on my path."
Psalm 119:105 (NIV)

Equally important is the study of the Bible—the living, breathing Word of God. In its pages, find the blueprint for a life rooted in Christ. By immersing ourselves in the teachings of the Bible, we gain insights into God's character, His plan for humanity, and how we can align our lives with His purposes. In Psalms 119:105, we find the imagery of God's Word as a guiding light, illuminating our path and providing direction for our lives. Just as a lamp guides our steps in darkness, the Word of God shines the way forward in our spiritual journey. Regular and intentional study gives us insights into God's will and purpose. The Bible becomes a well of wisdom, offering practical guidance for navigating life's problems and uncertainties. Becoming rooted in Christ involves immersing ourselves in the truths found in the pages of Scripture.

"All Scripture is God-breathed and is useful for teaching, rebuking, correcting and training in righteousness, so that the servant of God may be thoroughly equipped for every good work." 2 Timothy 3:16-17 (NIV)

The Bible, as the inspired Word of God, serves as spiritual nourishment. In these verses from 2 Timothy, we are reminded of the multifaceted role of Scripture in shaping our lives—teaching, rebuking, correcting, and training us in righteousness. Engaging with God's Word is not merely an academic exercise but a life-changing journey that equips us for the good works God has prepared for us. As we engage in

Scripture, we partake in a divine feast that nourishes our souls and encounters God's intentions. The Bible is a living, dynamic guide that provides wisdom for life's decisions, corrects our missteps, convicts our hearts, and aligns us with God's standards. Emerging into the Bible becomes a channel through which our relationship with Christ is nurtured and strengthened.

Significance of Worship

"Yet a time is coming and has now come when the true worshipers will worship the Father in the Spirit and in truth, for they are the kind of worshipers the Father seeks."

John 4:23 (NIV)

Worship, too, plays a crucial role in building our spiritual foundation. In the Gospel of John, Jesus emphasizes the basis of worship—authenticity and truth. It is not confined to a Sunday service but extends into our daily lives. Worship is a posture of the heart, an acknowledgment of God's greatness, and a celebration of His love. Worship is also an expression of humility and awe, acknowledging God as our Maker and Shepherd. When we approach God authentically, laying bare our hearts in adoration and surrender, we enter communion with the Father. Jesus invites us into a deeper dimension of worship—one that goes beyond the flesh and engages the Spirit. Whether through communal gatherings or personal moments of adoration, worship is vital in solidifying our foundation in Christ. As we learn to worship in Spirit and in truth, our connection with Christ deepens, and our spiritual foundation is enriched. Worship strengthens our faith by reminding us of God's care and our identity as His beloved. As we engage in heartfelt worship, our faith is strengthened, and our relationship with Christ deepens, creating a space for intimacy and transformation in the presence of our loving God.

Chapter Three

Knowing the Character of God

Understanding God's character provides a framework for trust and confidence in His nature. In times of uncertainty, adversity, or doubt, the knowledge that God is loving, faithful, and sovereign becomes a pillar. This understanding empowers us to navigate life's challenges with resilience, hope, and confidence, knowing that we serve a God whose character remains constant and reliable. When we truly grasp these truths, it transforms how we view ourselves, others, and the world around us. *Proverbs 3:5-6* advises, *"Trust in the Lord with all your heart and lean not on your own understanding; in all your ways submit to him, and he will make your paths straight."* Such trust is nurtured through awareness of God's character.

Understanding God's Love

"But God demonstrates his own love for us in this: While we were still sinners, Christ died for us." Romans 5:8 (NIV)

The love of God is a foundational aspect of being rooted in Christ. It goes beyond simply knowing that God loves us; it involves comprehending His love's depth, breadth, and unconditional nature. When we truly understand God's love, it transforms our relationship with him and how we view ourselves and others. God's love is not based on our performance or worthiness. It is a love that surpasses human understanding and extends to every person, regardless of past mistakes or current circumstances. This means that no matter what we have done or how far we may have strayed from Him, His love remains constant and unwavering. The Bible tells us that *"God demonstrates his own love for us in this: While we were still sinners, Christ died for us" (Romans 5:8).* This act of selfless love shows us that there is nothing we can do to earn or deserve God's love; it is freely given to us. When we face trials or hardships, it can be easy to question whether God truly loves us. However, knowing the magnitude of his love allows us to fasten our faith in the unshakable assurance that God's love is not contingent on our circumstances. Understanding the depth of His love provides a solid foundation upon which we can stand firm, even in the face of adversity. The knowledge that God's love is vast, enduring, and unconditional becomes a wellspring of comfort, reminding us that we are not alone in our struggles. Understanding God's love also empowers us to extend that same love to others. Jesus commanded His followers to *"love one another as I have loved you" (John 13:34)*. When we grasp the depth of God's love for us, it compels us to show that same kind of sacrificial and unconditional love towards those around us. The love of God has the power to transform lives and bring healing to broken relationships.

Trusting in God's Faithfulness

"He is the rock; his works are perfect, and all his ways are just. A faithful God who does no wrong, upright and just is he." Deuteronomy 32:4 (NIV)

Trusting in God's faithfulness is another crucial aspect of being rooted in Christ. It involves relying on Him entirely, even when circumstances seem uncertain or overwhelming. When you trust in God's faithfulness, you acknowledge that He is always faithful to His promises and will never abandon us. God has a tried, tested, and proven track record that shows he can never fail and will never fail. The Bible is filled with accounts of how God remained faithful to His people, even when they were unfaithful. For example, despite the Israelites' repeated disobedience and rebellion, God continued to provide for them, protect them, and guide them toward the Promised Land. In our lives, trusting in God's faithfulness means believing He will fulfill His promises to us. This requires patience and perseverance, especially when it seems like those promises are taking longer than expected or when obstacles arise. However, we can find assurance in knowing that *"God is not human, that he should lie, not a human being, that he should change his mind" (Numbers 23:19)*. What he has spoken will come to pass. Trusting in God's faithfulness also means surrendering our plans and desires to His will. It requires letting go of control and trusting that His ways are higher and better than ours *(Isaiah 5:8-9)*. This can be challenging, especially when we have our own ideas of how things should unfold. However, when we trust God's faithfulness, we open ourselves to experiencing His perfect plan for our lives. The story of

Joseph from the Old Testament is an excellent example of an individual who faced seemingly insurmountable predicaments but chose to trust God anyway. Despite being sold into slavery by his own brothers and enduring years of hardship and injustice, Joseph remained faithful to God and eventually rose to a position of significant influence in Egypt. Through it all, he trusted that God had a purpose for his life and that he would fulfill His promises. Trusting in God's faithfulness also involves seeking Him through prayer and relying on His guidance. We can turn to him for wisdom and direction when we face difficult decisions or uncertainties. The more we cultivate a relationship with Him through prayer, the more we recognize His voice and trust in His leadership.

Recognizing God's Sovereignty

"I make known the end from the beginning, from ancient times, what is still to come. I say, 'My purpose will stand, and I will do all that I please." Isaiah 46:10 (NIV)

Recognizing God's sovereignty is paramount in the life of a believer as it instills a profound sense of trust and surrender. Acknowledging that God is sovereign means understanding He is in absolute control over all things — both in the universe and the intricate details of our lives. This awareness provides comfort and security, especially amid uncertainty and challenges. When we encounter situations beyond our control, we can find peace in knowing that nothing catches God by surprise. In *Isaiah 46:10*, the Lord declares, *"I make known the end from the beginning, from ancient times, what is still to come. I say, 'My purpose will stand, and I will do all that I please."* God has authority and control over the unfolding of history and the fulfillment of His purposes. Recognizing God's sovereignty leads to a shift in perspective. It allows us to release the burden of trying to control every aspect of our lives and instead embrace a posture of humble submission. Recognizing God's sovereignty also means understanding that He is not limited by time or space. He exists outside our human constraints and simultaneously sees the beginning and the end. This allows Him to work all things together for good, even in hopeless or chaotic situations *(Romans 8:28)*. Trusting in God's sovereignty means acknowledging His wisdom and understanding that His plans are far greater than ours. *Proverbs 19:21* reflects this sentiment: *"Many are the plans in a person's heart, but it is the Lord's purpose that prevails."* By recognizing God's sovereignty, we can navigate life with a sense of peace, knowing we are under the loving and purposeful guidance of a God who holds the entire universe in His hands. Take time to reflect on your own experiences and look for instances where you have seen God's sovereignty at work, even under challenging circumstances.

Chapter Four

Face Trials With Christ

Facing the trials of life with Christ is an intimate journey where we find refuge, strength, and purpose in adversity. It involves a partnership where faith, anchored in the promises of God, becomes the catalyst for perseverance and transformation. This journey reshapes the narrative of trials, viewing them as opportunities to draw closer to Christ, experience His sustaining grace, and emerge victorious in life's tribulations.

The Storms of Life

"In this world, you will have trouble. But take heart! I have overcome the world." John 16:33 (NIV)

Embracing the reality of storms as inevitable challenges is essential to the Christian journey. Jesus, in His profound wisdom, prepares us followers for the trials and tribulations they will inevitably face in this world. John 16:33 serves as both an acknowledgment and a comforting reassurance. Troubles will come; storms will arise. Yet, we are called to take heart in the face of adversity. The assurance that Jesus has overcome the world becomes a source of hope and resilience. It transforms the perspective on challenges, shifting the focus from despair to the triumph found in Christ. Navigating storms with faith involves recognizing the certainty of trials while remaining secure in the ultimate victory won by our Savior. Face adversity not with fear but with a profound trust in the One who has conquered the storms we encounter.

Anchored in Faith

"Now faith is confidence in what we hope for and assurance about what we do not see." Hebrews 1:1 (NIV)

Faith serves as the anchor in our journey—a secure foundation that sustains us through life's storms. It's not a one-time event but a continual exercise of trust, confidence, and reliance on the promises of God. Being anchored in faith means finding confidence in the unseen aspects of our spiritual journey. It involves trusting in the goodness of God's character, even when His workings are not immediately apparent. This confidence is not rooted in our abilities or understanding but in the unchanging nature of God Himself. The ongoing exercise of faith propels us forward in our journey. Faith is not a hindrance but a driving force that enables us to move forward even when the path ahead seems unclear. It is a transformative exercise that empowers us to take steps of obedience, to endure in times of trial, and to hope against all odds, knowing that the God in whom we place our faith is faithful. Our faith is not based on wishful thinking but on the trustworthiness of God. The anchor of faith finds its strength in the unchanging and reliable nature of the One in whom we have placed our trust.

Overcoming Doubt

> *"Immediately the boy's father exclaimed, "I do believe; help me overcome my unbelief!" Mark 9:24*

In *Mark 9:24*, a father cries out to Jesus, saying, *"I believe; help my unbelief!"* This plea encapsulates the tension and vulnerability that often characterizes the human experience of faith. The man's acknowledgment of both belief and unbelief reflects the nature of faith, acknowledging that, despite genuine trust, doubts can still linger. This honest expression captures the struggles we face in navigating our journey of faith. It also highlights the Father's humility, recognizing his need for divine assistance in overcoming the doubts that threaten to overshadow his belief. Jesus does not rebuke the Father for his admission of doubt; instead, He responds with understanding and healing. This interaction emphasizes the gracious nature of God, who meets His children in their moments of vulnerability and provides the support needed to overcome doubt. It encourages us to bring our uncertainties before God, trusting His response is one of love and assistance. Instead of concealing doubts, the verse encourages an open dialogue with God about the complexities of our faith.

Overcoming doubts as a child of God involves a multifaceted approach that combines spiritual, intellectual, and relational elements. Regular prayer, studying Scripture, and cultivating a personal relationship with God are crucial to building a solid faith foundation. Seeking guidance through prayerful reflection and meditating on passages that affirm God's promises and character can help counter doubts. Additionally, surrounding oneself with a supportive community of believers provides encouragement and accountability. Sharing doubts with fellow believers and engaging in open discussions can offer perspectives, insights, and testimonies that reinforce faith and dispel uncertainties.

It is paramount to overcome doubts as a child of God because doubts can erode the foundation of faith and hinder spiritual growth. If left unaddressed, doubt can lead to detachment from God, robbing us of peace, joy, and purpose. Overcoming doubts fosters an intimate, more mature faith that can withstand life's inevitable pitfalls. Approach God with humility, trusting He can turn moments of doubt into opportunities for strengthened faith and encounters with His mercy and grace.

Chapter Five

Identity Established In God

The identity established in God is one grounded in purpose, significance, and unshakable worth. It provides a stable and unchanging foundation in the midst of life's uncertainties. When external factors like achievements, relationships, or societal expectations fluctuate, the unshakable identity in God remains a constant source of affirmation. This identity is a lens through which we perceive ourselves, reminding us that we are loved, valued, and purposefully created. A God-established identity fosters resilience in the face of adversities, as it grounds us in an eternal perspective that surpasses the temporal struggles of this world.

Embracing Your Status as Children of God

In John 1:12, it is declared, *"But to all who did receive him, who believed in his name, he gave the right to become children of God."* This verse encapsulates the nature of faith, highlighting that through acceptance and belief in Christ, we are granted the privilege of becoming God's children. This truth shapes our identity by establishing a familial bond with the Almighty, emphasizing that our significance is derived from being part of His eternal family. When we accept Jesus as our Savior, we are adopted into God's family and become His beloved children.

Understanding that you are a child of God means recognizing that you have a loving Father who cares deeply for you. Just as earthly parents provide for the needs of their children, our Heavenly Father promises to meet all our needs according to His riches in glory (Philippians 4:19). He is always there to comfort, guide, and protect us. As a child of God, you also have the privilege of intimate relationships with Him. We can confidently approach Him and pour our hearts into Him in prayer. He listens attentively to every word we say and delights in spending time with us. This relationship isn't based solely on performance or merit but on His grace and love for us.

Embracing your status as a child of God means understanding that you have been given a new identity in Christ. You are no longer defined by our past mistakes or failures but by who God says we are. You are forgiven, redeemed, and made new in Him *(2 Corinthians 5:17)*. To fully embrace your status as children of God, you must renew your mind with the truth of Scripture. The Bible is filled with verses affirming our identity in Christ and reminding us of the incredible love God has lavished upon us *(1 John 3:1)*. Meditating on these truths helps combat the lies and doubts that may undermine your confidence in who you are in Him.

One practical way to embrace your status as children of God is by declaring the word of God over yourself and your situations. Speaking the Bible aloud reinforces Scripture in your heart and mind while reminding God of his word concerning you. For example, you can declare, "I am a child of God, deeply loved and accepted by Him. I am chosen, forgiven, and set free from the bondage of sin. I have been given a purpose and a hope in Christ." These declarations serve as powerful reminders of your true identity. Embracing your status as children of God is crucial for living out your faith with confidence and joy. It means recognizing that we have a loving Father who cares for us deeply, understanding our new identity in Christ, renewing our minds with the truth of Scripture, and declaring His Word. When we fully embrace our status as children of God, we can walk in the freedom and victory that He has provided us.

Co-Heirs with Christ

Understanding that you are co-heirs with Christ is a profound truth that transforms how you view yourself and your relationship with God. As co-heirs, we share in all the blessings and inheritance Jesus received from the Father.

It is helpful to consider what it means to be an heir to grasp the significance of being co-heirs with Christ. In earthly terms, an heir receives an inheritance from their parents or ancestors. This inheritance often includes material possessions or wealth passed down through generations. In the spiritual realm, as co-heirs with Christ, we inherit God's abundant blessings and promises. These include eternal life, the forgiveness of sins, the indwelling presence of the Holy Spirit, access to the Father through prayer, and the hope of glory *(Romans 8:17)*. We are no longer slaves to sin but have been set free to live as children of God.

Being co-heirs with Christ implies that we have a joint inheritance with Him. This means we are united in His victory over sin and death. We are called to reign with Him in His kingdom and share in His authority *(2 Timothy 2:12)*. This truth empowers us to walk boldly in our calling and fulfill the purpose that God has ordained for us. Recognizing that we are co-heirs with Christ is a transformative truth that impacts every aspect of our lives. It means singing in all the blessings and inheritance that Jesus received from the Father, enduring suffering for righteousness's sake, participating in His redemptive work, walking boldly in our calling, and extending grace and love to others. When you fully embrace your status as co-heirs with Christ, you can live with confidence, purpose, and a sense of belonging.

Finding Worth and Value in God Alone

In a world that often measures worth based on external achievements or the opinions of others, understanding that your value comes from God alone is liberating. When you find your worth and value in Him alone, you are freed from constantly striving for approval or validation from others. You no longer need to seek affirmation through worldly success or the accumulation of material possessions. Instead, you can rest assured that you are deeply loved and accepted by God, just as we are.

Finding worth and value in Christ alone is recognizing that your identity is not defined by what you do but by who you are in Christ. Your job title, academic achievements, or social status do not determine your worth. It is rooted in being created in the image of God and redeemed by the precious blood of Jesus *(Genesis 1:27; Ephesians 1:7)* that determines your worth. Understanding this truth helps us overcome feelings of inadequacy or comparison with others. You can celebrate the unique gifts and talents that God has given you without feeling the need to measure up to someone else's standards. You have been fearfully and wonderfully made for a specific purpose *(Psalm 139:14)*. Finding worth and value in Christ alone means recognizing that your worth is not based on your performance or good works. You cannot earn God's love or acceptance through your efforts. It is solely by His grace that we are saved and made righteous in Christ *(Ephesians 2:8-9)*.

Another aspect of finding worth and value in Him alone is understanding that your true identity is hidden in Christ. Our lives are now hidden with Christ in God *(Colossians 3:3)*. This means that your worth and value are secure because they are rooted in the unchanging nature of God, not in the shifting opinions or circumstances of this world. Finding worth and value in Him alone requires surrendering your desires, ambitions, and insecurities to God daily. It means seeking His approval above all else and aligning your thoughts and actions with His truth. When you prioritize pleasing God rather than seeking the approval of others, you can experience true freedom and joy.

Finding worth and value in Him alone is a truth that liberates us from the need for external validation or worldly achievements. It means recognizing that our identity is rooted in being created in the image of God, redeemed by Jesus' sacrifice, and hidden with Christ in God. When you find your worth and value in Him alone, you can live with confidence, contentment, and purpose.

Chapter Six

Embracing Your Unique Purpose

Embracing one's unique purpose lies in aligning one's life with God's divine intentions. Each individual is uniquely equipped to fulfill a specific role in God's overarching plan for creation. Embracing one's unique purpose is an act of obedience and trust in God's wisdom, acknowledging that He has crafted a personalized and meaningful role for each person to play in the grand narrative of His redemptive story. This alignment with divine purpose brings fulfillment and meaning to life as you discover the joy that comes from walking in harmony with God's intended design for our existence. As you recognize and live out your distinct purpose, it contributes to the overall health and vitality of the Church. Just as different parts of the body serve unique functions but work together in harmony, embracing your unique purposes contributes to the flourishing of the Christian community.

"For I know the plans I have for you, declares the Lord, plans to prosper you and not to harm you, plans to give you hope and a future."
Jeremiah 29:11 (NIV)

Your purpose is not haphazard or accidental. Instead, it is intricately woven into the fabric of God's intentional design for each of His children. The ultimate goal of God's purpose is articulated in the promise of hope and a future. Your purpose is not confined to the present moment; it extends into eternity. God's plans for you are forward-looking, offering a future filled with hope, promise, and a sense of destiny. Your purpose is not a mystery hidden from you but a revelation from a loving and intentional Creator. God's declaration, *"For I know the plans I have for you,"* resonates with a personalized assurance that your purpose is intricately tailored to our unique identities, gifts, and callings. Unpacking purpose involves recognizing the inherent goodness embedded in God's plans. His intentions are not to harm but to prosper, revealing a purpose far beyond our immediate circumstances.

"Trust in the Lord with all your heart and lean not on your own understanding; in all your ways submit to him, and he will make your paths straight." Proverbs 3:5-6 (NIV)

Discovering purpose involves deliberately surrendering your preconceived notions and trusting God's plans surpassing human comprehension. It encourages humility, acknowledging your need for divine insight in discerning the intricate details of our purpose. Trust becomes the bedrock on which the journey unfolds, admitting that God's understanding far surpasses our own limited perspectives. Seeking purpose is not a compartmentalized endeavor but an all-encompassing commitment to align every aspect of life with God's guidance. This submission involves surrendering personal desires, ambitions and plans to yield to the divine unfolding of purpose. Seeking God's will is not futile but a journey with a guaranteed destination. The promise implies that as we trust, relinquish self-reliance, and submit to God's will, He, in His faithfulness, will guide and direct our paths.

Proverbs 3:5-6 establishes seeking God's will as an essential step in aligning with one's unique purpose. By actively seeking God's will, we position ourselves to discern and embrace the distinctive purpose He has ordained for our lives. Seeking God's will is not a one-time event but a continual, lifelong journey. As we understand God's character and deepen our roots in Christ, seeking His will becomes an ongoing commitment.

Embracing one's unique purpose as a child of God is an act of stewardship. It involves recognizing the entrusted talents, resources, and opportunities given by God and using them for His glory and the well-being of others. It is a response to the love and grace extended by God as we seek to live out our purpose as an expression of gratitude and obedience. In embracing your unique purpose, you find personal fulfillment and contribute to the collective flourishing of God's kingdom on earth.

Chapter Seven

Manifestations of Spiritual Growth

(The Fruits of the Spirit)

As our roots in Christ grow more profound, they bear fruit—a visible and tangible expression of the power of the Spirit at work within us. In this chapter, we explore the concept of the fruit of the Spirit, understanding how spiritual growth results in the manifestation of these virtues in our lives. Each fruit is a testimony to the depth of our roots and the flourishing journey of being rooted in Christ.

"But the fruit of the Spirit is love, joy, peace, forbearance, kindness, goodness, faithfulness, gentleness, and self-control. Against such things, there is no law." Galatians 5:22-23 (NIV)

Love

Love stands at the forefront of the fruits of the Spirit, not by coincidence but by design. It serves as the foundational expression of our connection with Christ. This love transcends human understanding, encompassing selfless, sacrificial affection for others. It mirrors the divine love exemplified by Christ, becoming the cornerstone of spiritual growth. It influences how we treat others, respond to challenges, and engage with the world. A life rooted in Christ is characterized by love radiating through every aspect, significantly impacting those we encounter. Circumstances, relationships, or personal preferences do not limit it. Instead, it is a divine love infused by the Holy Spirit, which empowers us to love others unconditionally. As our roots in Christ deepen, this transcendent love becomes a defining characteristic of our lives. It goes beyond surface-level affection and delves into the depths of compassion and concern for others. As we grow in our rootedness in Christ, we increasingly exhibit a love that goes beyond sentiment, influencing our actions and relationships.

Joy

"You make known to me the path of life; you will fill me with joy in your presence, with eternal pleasures at your right hand." Psalm 16:11 (NIV)

Joy is derived from God; it is not found in the world's offerings but in the divine presence that illuminates the path toward a fulfilled and purposeful life. The joy of the Lord is not contingent on favorable or external circumstances. Instead, it remains a constant companion because it is rooted in something unchanging—God's presence. As we grow in our understanding and experience of God's presence, joy becomes a defining characteristic. It influences their perspective, allowing them to navigate life's complexities with gratitude and hope. Having joy is linked to being in the presence of God. When you are in the presence of God, you can experience a joy that emanates from an intimate and abiding relationship with the Creator, and it is a natural outflow of our connection with Christ. Joy is not a sporadic emotion but an integral part of the believer's demeanor. The growth in Christ is marked by an increasing awareness and appreciation of the joy that comes from walking in His presence.

Peace

"And the peace of God, which transcends all understanding, will guard your hearts and your minds in Christ Jesus."
Philippians 4:7 (NIV)

Peace originates from God. It is not a peace manufactured by human effort or external circumstances but a divine gift bestowed upon believers. The peace of God is not merely the absence of conflict but a profound and supernatural tranquility. The peace described in *Philippians 4:7* surpasses human comprehension. It defies logical explanation or rationalization. It is a peace that exists beyond the constraints of human intellect and is not subject to the flow of worldly circumstances. The peace of God serves as a guardian for the hearts and minds of believers. This peace is a protective force in a world filled with anxiety and uncertainty. It shields the innermost thoughts and emotions, providing a sanctuary of calmness amid the storms of life. As we grow in our spiritual journey, the experience of this peace intensifies. The more rooted one becomes in Christ, the more profound and tangible this peace becomes.

Forbearance (Patience)

"Be joyful in hope, be patient in affliction, faithful in prayer."

Romans 12:12 (NIV)

Forbearance goes beyond mere tolerance; it encompasses a spirit of patience and grace. Forbearance is a virtue that shapes character and fortifies faith. It represents the capacity to endure difficulties and persevere in faith. This Spirit of patience is a distinctive mark of believers growing in the fruit of forbearance. This patience is not passive resignation but an active trust in God's sovereignty and a recognition that trials are opportunities for spiritual growth. Spiritual growth manifests as believers learn to wait on God's timing, trusting His plans despite uncertainties. Patience becomes a virtue that shapes their character, fostering resilience in the face of trials.

Kindness and Goodness

"Be kind and compassionate to one another, forgiving each other, just as in Christ God forgave you." Ephesians 4:32

(NIV)

The call to "be kind and compassionate" is framed within God's lavish grace. Kindness, in this sense, is not merely a moral duty but a responsive expression of the kindness and compassion that God has abundantly poured out on us. It is a natural outflow of the grace that has touched and transformed our lives. As we deepen our roots in Christ, we experience God's goodness and become vessels through which His goodness is expressed to others. Being rooted in Christ involves receiving and radiating God's goodness into the world. This aligns with the biblical narrative calling believers to be ambassadors of God's love and goodness. As individuals grow spiritually, they exhibit kindness, demonstrating a genuine concern for others' well-being. Kindness and goodness manifest as believers mature in their rootedness, expressing Christ-like virtues in their daily interactions.

Faithfulness

"Now it is required that those who have been given a trust must prove faithful." 1 Corinthians 4:2 (NIV)

Trust is the foundational element of faithfulness. Trust is not merely a passive reliance but an active and intentional placing of confidence in God. The call to faith is rooted in the understanding that believers have been entrusted with responsibilities, gifts, and a relationship with God, and this trust requires a faithful response. The phrase "must prove faithful" implies an ongoing and active demonstration of faithfulness. It involves living out the trust placed in believers by God. This proving of faith is not just a one-time event but a continuous commitment to stewardship—responsibly managing and utilizing the resources and gifts entrusted to them by God. Trust extends beyond a vertical relationship with God to horizontal relationships with others. Faithfulness in relationships involves being reliable, trustworthy, and loyal. It reflects the character of God, who is faithful in His covenantal relationships with His people. We are called to mirror the same faithfulness as God in all of our relationships. This involves a consistent commitment to spiritual disciplines, such as prayer, studying God's Word, and participating in the community of faith. This consistency reflects a faithfulness that withstands the tests of time and circumstance.

Gentleness

"Therefore, as God's chosen people, holy, and dearly loved, clothes yourselves with compassion, kindness, humility, gentleness, and patience" Colossians 3:12 (NIV)

Gentleness, as a fruit of the Spirit, is not a product of human effort or personality but a result of the Holy Spirit's presence and work within the believer. It is a quality that reflects the character of Christ, who is described as *"gentle and humble in heart" (Matthew 11:29)*. The presence of gentleness often indicates spiritual maturity. It involves a depth of character that goes beyond external behaviors to the heart attitude. A mature believer, rooted in Christ, exhibits gentleness as a natural outflow of the internal transformation the Holy Spirit brings. Gentleness is closely tied to humility. A gentle spirit recognizes its dependence on God, acknowledging that all strength and goodness come from Him. This humility prevents arrogance or harshness and fosters an attitude of meekness characterized by strength under control. Gentleness does not exist in isolation but is intertwined with the other fruits of the Spirit mentioned in *Galatians 5:22-23*. It complements love, kindness, and patience, contributing to the overall bouquet of virtues that mark a Spirit-filled life. As we become rooted in Christ, gentleness becomes a natural and evident expression of the work of the Holy Spirit within us.

Self-Control

"Like a city whose walls are broken through is a person who lacks self-control." Proverbs 25:28 (NIV)

The analogy of a city with broken walls emphasizes the vulnerability of a person who lacks self-control. In ancient times, city walls were critical for defense, protecting inhabitants from external threats. Likewise, self-control serves as a spiritual fortification, guarding us against the influences that may compromise our spiritual well-being. Self-control is not achieved through sheer willpower alone but is a result of the work of the Holy Spirit within the believer. It manifests God's power, enabling us to exercise discipline over our desires and actions. Self-control involves disciplined living and the ability to exercise restraint. It encompasses various aspects of life, including thoughts, words, and actions. The disciplined individual, rooted in Christ, is empowered to make choices aligned with God's principles, resisting the allure of instant gratification or harmful influences.

A lack of self-control exposes you to spiritual erosion, allowing harmful influences to infiltrate and undermine your faith. Self-control becomes a defensive measure, protecting the integrity of one's spiritual life and preserving the foundation rooted in Christ. Just as the health of a tree is contingent on the strength of its roots, the vitality of a believer's spiritual life is closely linked to the presence of self-control. By guarding against impulsive or detrimental behaviors, self-control ensures that the roots of faith, love, and obedience remain strong and nourished. The ultimate model of self-control is found in the life of Jesus Christ. His ability to resist temptation, focus on His mission, and submit to the Father's will exemplifies perfect self-control. Believers, as they deepen their roots in Christ, seek to emulate His example, allowing the Spirit to cultivate the fruit of self-control in our lives.

The fruits of the Spirit are not just virtues to aspire to but tangible manifestations of spiritual growth. These qualities—love, joy, peace, patience, kindness, goodness, faithfulness, gentleness, and self-control—bear witness to the profound impact of your connection with Christ. As you nurture your rootedness in Christ, these fruits become evident in your character, influencing your actions, attitudes, and relationships. May the manifestation of these fruits be a source of inspiration and encouragement on your continuing journey of spiritual growth.

Chapter Eight

The Ripple Effect of a Rooted Life

Displaying Christ

"You are the salt of the earth..." *Matthew 5:13 (NIV)*

Just as salt enhances the flavor of food, our presence as children of God is meant to enrich and bring a unique savor and transformation to the world. Salt is also a preservative, preventing decay and spoilage. Similarly, we are to act as preservatives in the world, standing against moral decay and upholding righteousness. A life deeply rooted in Christ catalyzes positive change in the world. This chapter delves into the expansive ripple effect that emanates from a life firmly grounded in the teachings and love of Christ. As we comprehend the significance of our rootedness, we unearth the power to influence and illuminate the world with the love and grace we've received.

A life rooted in Christ generates a profound ripple effect beyond personal transformation. This ripple effect begins with the internal change, as the fruits of the Spirit—love, joy, peace, patience, kindness, goodness, faithfulness, gentleness, and self-control—naturally manifest in our character and interactions. As these qualities flourish within, they inevitably spill over into the surrounding community, creating an atmosphere of grace, compassion, and authenticity. The initial impact of a rooted life is witnessed in our transformed character and conduct, serving as a tangible testimony to the substantial power of Christ. The love we receive from Christ becomes a wellspring that overflows, touching the lives of those around us. Joy becomes infectious, spreading a contagious enthusiasm for life. Peace becomes a stabilizing force, influencing relationships and fostering harmony. Relationships are infused with a depth of meaning and forgiveness, reflecting the selfless and sacrificial love modeled by Christ. This ripple effect creates a community of compassion, empathy, and a shared commitment to live out the principles of Christ.

Beyond personal and relational spheres, the impact of a rooted life resonates on a broader scale. Like a city set on a hill, a life grounded in Christ becomes a beacon of hope and inspiration for others. The inward transformation journey radiates outward, influencing communities, workplaces, and societal structures. Acts of kindness, expressions of love, and a commitment to justice become the building blocks of positive change. The ripple effect has the potential to transform the world, creating waves of compassion, grace, and transformative influence that reach far beyond your immediate circle. In this way, a life rooted in Christ becomes a catalyst for a broader, enduring impact that reflects the redemptive power of the Gospel.

Chapter Nine

The Journey Continues

Rooted & Growing

In this final chapter, as we embrace the richness of being rooted in Christ, anchored in faith, and continuously flourishing, we step into a future marked by hope and purpose. The journey extends into the horizon of possibilities, beckoning us to walk with anticipation and gratitude for the grace that has accompanied us thus far. Acknowledging the ongoing nature of this spiritual expedition is an essential aspect of the concluding chapter. It prompts us to recognize that the journey does not end with the turning of the last page but extends into our everyday lifestyles. Being rooted in Christ is a daily practice, an intentional choice to align your life with the teachings and example of Jesus. This journey is an open door, an ongoing call to embrace the richness of a life rooted in Christ.

Reflecting on the Transformative Journey

To reflect on this transformative journey is to take a deliberate pause, step back, and observe the intricate patterns that have emerged as a result of your walk with Christ. In the process of reflection, we can trace the hand of God in every season of our lives. The obstacles that seemed insurmountable, the joys that felt transcendent, and the moments of profound connection with God—all are threads meticulously woven into the fabric of our spiritual journey. Through reflection, we discern the divine craftsmanship at work, shaping us into vessels of His grace. The good work initiated by God in our lives is not a fleeting endeavor. It's a continuous commitment from the Creator to His creation. The journey of transformation is not a solitary endeavor but a collaborative work between God and the heart that is yielded.

The Ongoing Nature of Spiritual Growth

The concept of spiritual growth is not a motionless destination but a perpetual expedition. This lifelong adventure invites us to embark on a continuous journey of discovery, transformation, and deepening intimacy with Christ. To embrace the ongoing nature of spiritual growth is to acknowledge that the path of discipleship is ever-unfolding. Don't settle in complacency but venture into the uncharted territories of our faith. The call is to go deeper, to seek with a hunger for understanding, and to learn with a heart open to the revelations that each stage of the journey brings. Embracing the ongoing nature of spiritual growth is a commitment—an intentional choice to cultivate a relationship with Christ. This commitment involves a continual posture of humility, acknowledging that there is always more to discover about the inexhaustible depths of God's grace. The journey is not confined to a specific time frame but is a continual, lifelong pursuit. It unfolds in the daily moments of seeking, learning, and evolving. This journey leads to a deeper and more profound relationship with Christ, with the ultimate aim of bringing glory to His name.

Committing to a Life Rooted in Christ

Commitment is the pillar that keeps us grounded in Christ, irrespective of the shifting tides and storms that life may bring. This commitment is not a one-time decision but a continuous, daily surrender. It doesn't end when you give your life to Christ. Your commitment to Christ is a root that draws sustenance from Him, providing stability in the face of life's uncertainties. The natural outcome of commitment is being strengthened in the faith. It is a byproduct of a life lived in daily surrender to Christ—a continual refinement and maturation process. This commitment ensures that our faith does not remain stagnant but is resilient and able to withstand the tests that come our way. A life rooted in Christ is a multifaceted journey involving intentional choices and daily surrender.

Continuously Flourishing

A life rooted in Christ transcends mere survival—it speaks to a life that thrives, blooms, and bears fruit in abundance. It's a vibrant existence marked by the continual manifestation of the fruits of the Spirit and an impact that extends beyond personal growth to influence the world around us. A life rooted in Christ will flourish and bear fruit, staying fresh and green even in the later seasons of life.

In concluding our journey, we recognize that being rooted in Christ is an ongoing, transformative experience. It's a commitment to reflect on the past, embrace the present, and anticipate the future with hope and faith. As we stand firm avering truth of God's Word, our lives become a testament to the continuous flourishing that occurs when we remain rooted and growing in Christ. May this journey be marked by grace, wisdom, and an ever-deepening connection with our Lord and Savior, Jesus Christ, forever and ever. Amen.

Made in the USA
Columbia, SC
08 April 2025

56278924R00035